Am I Going to Die?

**Sheila Hollins and Irene Tuffrey-Wijne
illustrated by Lisa Kopper**

D1099324

Books Beyond Words
RCPsych Publications/St George's, University of London
LONDON

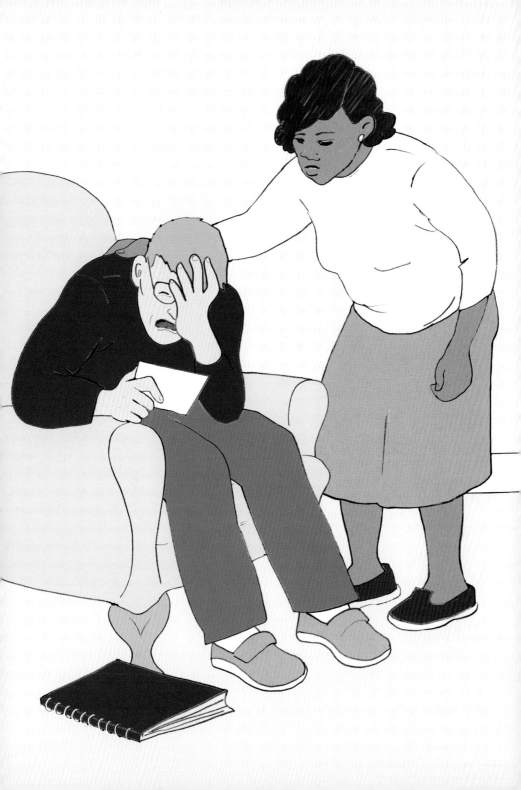

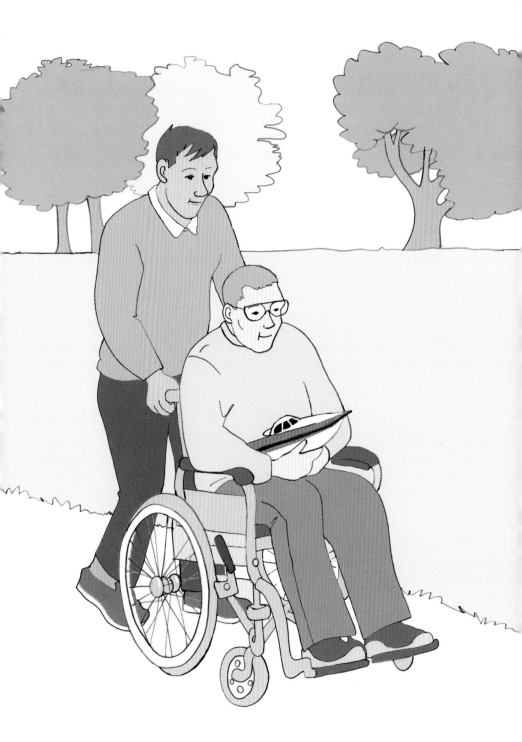

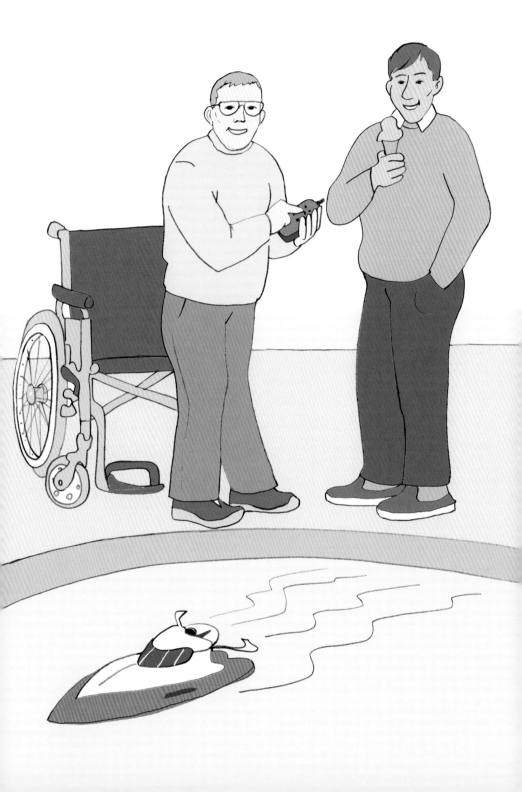

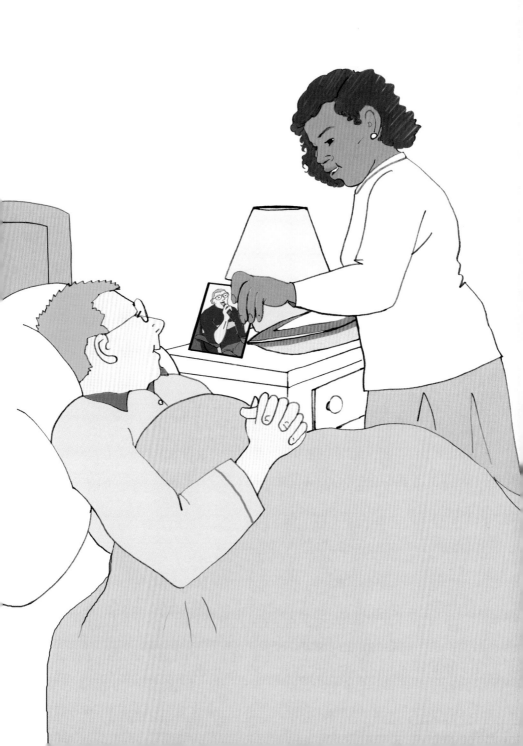

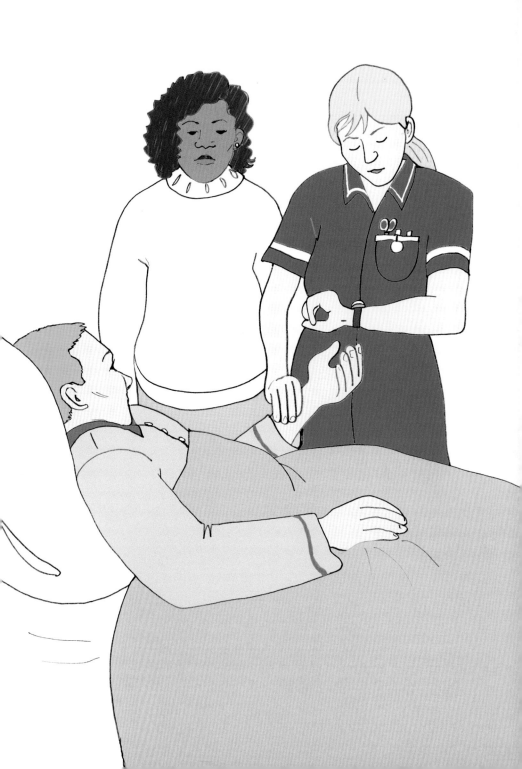

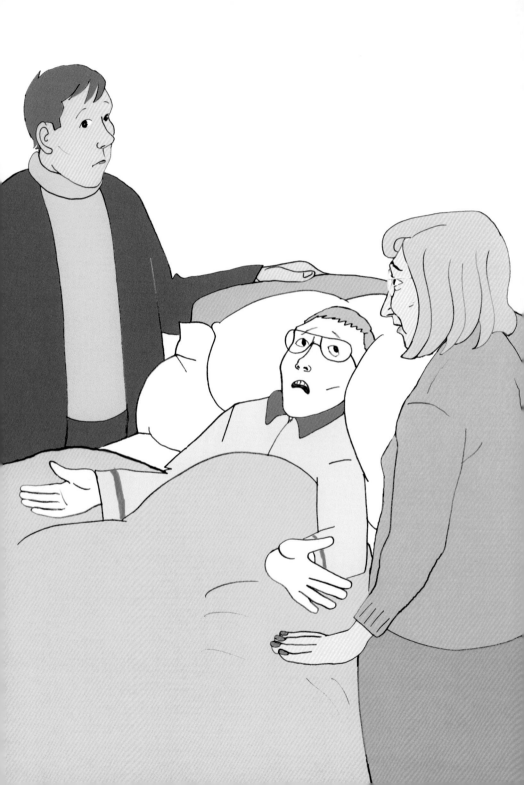

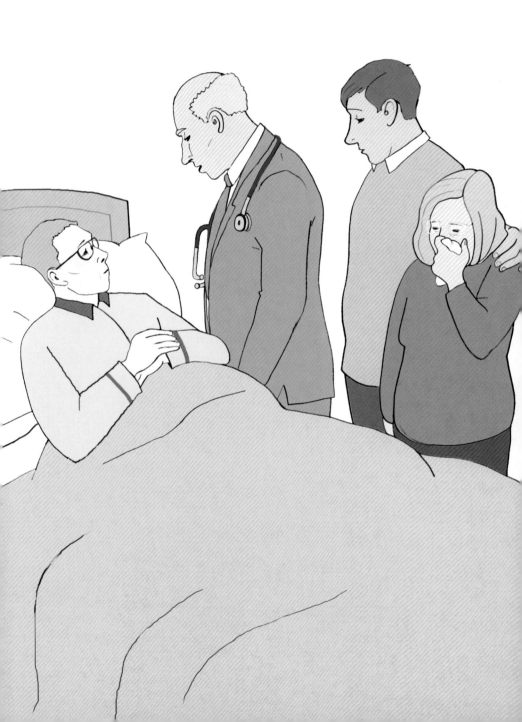

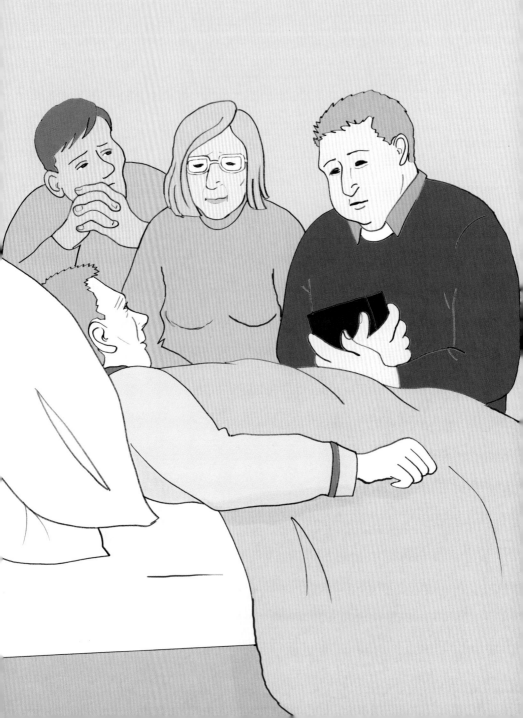

37

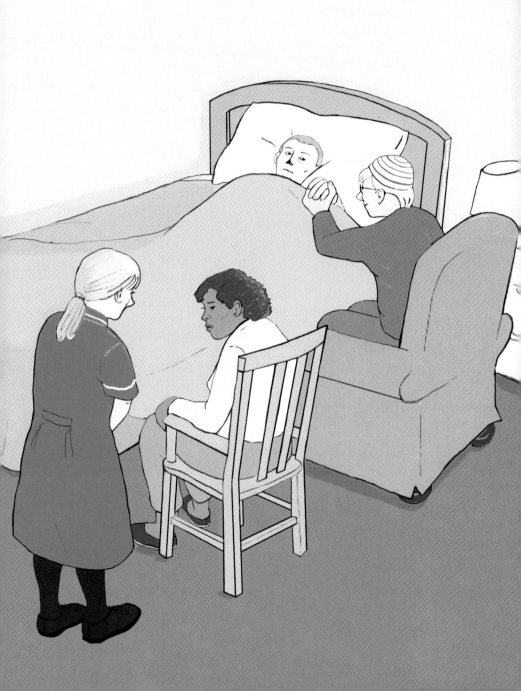

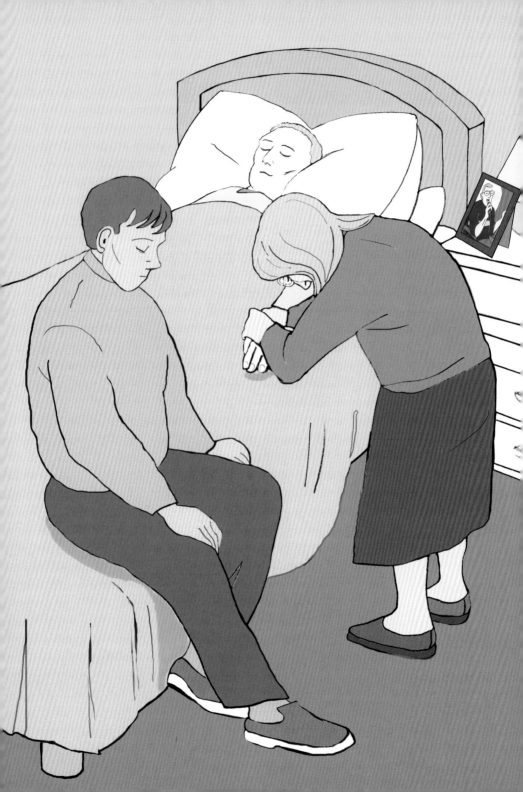

How to use this book

Here are some ideas we have found useful:

1. Read the book yourself. First, look through the pictures, then read the text. Choose the parts that are most appropriate for the person you are supporting.
2. Sit down beside the person you are supporting, and offer them the first picture you have chosen. Allow the person plenty of time to follow the pictures at his or her own pace. Don't feel you have to use the whole book in one sitting.
3. Depending on the response of the person you are supporting, prompt them to say what is happening:

   Who do you think that is?
   What are they doing?
   What is happening?
   Has that happened to you?
   How is he feeling? Do you feel like that?

   This will help you to judge how much the person has understood.

4. Provide as much support and reassurance as is needed by the person you are supporting, and answer their questions honestly.

The following words are provided for readers or carers who want a ready-made story rather than tell their own

1. John and Dorothy enjoy some tea together.

2. The doctor comes to John's house. Is John sick?

3. The doctor checks John's tummy. Dorothy stands and watches.

4. The doctor gives John a prescription.

5. John goes to the chemist to get his medicine.

6. John is really not well! It looks like he has got a tummy pain. Dorothy looks worried.

7. He sits on a bench in the street. He rests for a bit. Dorothy says there is no need to hurry.

8. Back home John sleeps in his chair. Dorothy puts the shopping away.

9. John still enjoys his food.

10. He likes looking at photos.

11. He looks at photos of his family. He looks at pictures of himself as a child. There are some pictures of him singing with friends.

12. John shows his favourite photos to Dorothy.

13. Oh dear. Something has upset John. Something in one of the pictures.

14. Dorothy rings John's Mum and says he is upset.

15. John tells his Mum what upset him. I wonder what upset him?

16. Mum comforts him. He looks calm now.

17. John's brother and his Mum come to see him. He is so pleased to see them!

18. John shows them his photos. They remember lots of happy times. John looks at a picture of a boating lake.

19. He goes out with his brother, but he can't walk far any more. He is in a wheelchair and carries a small boat.

20. They laugh a lot. John uses a remote control to sail the boat in the pond.

21. John goes to bed happy. He puts the boat next to his bed.

22. He has an accident in the night. He wets the bed. He is upset about it. Dorothy says it's OK.

23. The district nurse brings John a commode. It's for when he can't get to the toilet on time.

24. John is puzzled about the commode. The nurse says he can try it.

25. Some friends come to see John. They look fun! One has got a microphone. They want him to go out singing.

26. John asks Dorothy 'What do you think? I want to go singing with my friends. I don't want to stay in bed'.

27. John goes to karaoke. He loves singing. He is with his friends. Dorothy has come too. She takes a photo.

28. Now he is in bed. Dorothy shows him a picture – the one taken at karaoke!

29. John looks really ill. The nurse checks his pulse. Is he going to die?

30. His Mum and brother visit him. They look worried.

31. John asks them what's wrong with him.

32. 'Please tell me' he says. 'Am I going to die? I don't want to die.'

33. His Mum says he is going to die. She comforts him.

34. The doctor comes and talks to them. He answers their questions.

35. A priest comes to see John.

36. He prays with John and his family.

37. Mum hugs John. His family stays with him a lot of the time now.

38. John's friends come – they bring flowers. They are very quiet. They don't want to disturb him.

39. They sit quietly beside John's bed. No singing now! Just time to say goodbye.

40. John's Mum and brother sit and wait. John is dying.

41. John has died. He looks peaceful. Mum holds his hand. John's Mum and brother feel very sad.

Introduction

This book is based on 'The Veronica Project', a study of people with learning disabilities, ten of whom were terminally ill. The story in this book draws on their experiences of what was important for them when they were ill and dying. We are very grateful for their contribution, and that of their families, friends and carers. In particular, we would like to acknowledge the inspiration of John Davies, who was one of the people in 'The Veronica Project'. John knew he was dying. He said:

> 'I would like to make my story into a book. It should be told in a simple way so that people with learning disabilities can understand it. I want to say: This is my story, and I hope you see the funny side of things, but if it makes you sad, then I'm sorry. It's not all daffodils and tulips, there are some bad times, but I hope the good times outweigh the bad times.'

John Davies died in 2006. His photographs were used by Lisa Kopper, the illustrator, to help create the character of 'John' in this book.

Guide for supporters

Supporters are the people whom individuals trust and feel safe with when they are ill. They can be parents or other family members, friends or advocates, social care staff or healthcare professionals.

This book is designed for people with learning disabilities whose health is deteriorating and who are going to die. They could have cancer, or Alzheimer's disease, or any other illness that shortens their life; or maybe they don't have any particular diagnosis, but are getting close to dying because of old age. The book will also be useful for people with learning disabilities whose friend or relative is dying.

Supporting someone who is terminally ill is very demanding. As a supporter, you are likely to be close to the person who is dying. You care for them deeply and you want to do the best you can, but often you may not know what to do for the best. You may be sad and upset yourself. This book will help you to give the person good support.

We have spent many years working with people with learning disabilities who are ill and dying, and we have learnt a lot about what is important to them. The story in this book shows the physical process of getting more and more ill, but it also shows the emotional upsets, and how these can be supported. In our story, John is supported to live and die at home, but the book is also relevant if someone dies somewhere else, like a hospital. What matters is that you are focused on what is best for the person and what is possible, given the circumstances.

The pictures are designed to help the reader make sense of what is happening to them or the person they know who is ill. They help them to ask questions and to tell their own story, or express their own concerns. Or you could let the person you are supporting tell their own story. You may want to give the person the whole book to look at, or you could choose just a few pictures that you think will be particularly relevant. For example:

- A number of pictures are concerned with the physical process of getting more and more ill. For example, having the doctor visit, getting more tired throughout the book, needing a commode and a wheelchair, and finally being bed-bound. These can be used to help explain to the person what is happening to them.
- Some pictures are concerned with the emotional impact of terminal illness. For example, the need to look back and remember one's life, to see the people that mattered most, to enjoy some good times, and to say goodbye. These pictures can help you find out what the person's worries and wishes are.

Making choices

When someone's health is deteriorating, they may need to make some difficult choices. How can their increased dependency needs be met? What are their personal wishes and priorities? You will have to find this out from them. Many people will want to stay at home, with the people they know best. Is this possible? Can their carers cope? Some people will actually feel safer and happier in an environment where their increased nursing needs can be better supported, like a nursing home or hospice. But they will probably want to be somewhere close to home so that friends and family can visit them.

The most important question you need to ask is: 'What matters most to this person?' For example, who are the people they want to have around them? How would they like to spend their time? A night out at the karaoke club might exhaust them completely – is it worth it? (It may well be!) Could they still go to their favourite day activities, even if it's only for an hour and all they can do is sit and watch? What makes them feel safe?

Families and friends

Families are likely to be very important. Even if family members have not visited regularly, it is still essential to inform and involve them. Daily carers (paid staff) may quite often feel they know the person best, but families have known them longest, from the day they were born; those bonds of belonging can never be dismissed, and often become crucial at the end of life. If families and daily carers can work well together, it will greatly benefit the person, as it did in John's story.

It is also a good idea to involve friends. Sometimes, supporters are not sure what to tell other people with learning disabilities if someone is dying. It is usually best to be open and honest. 'John is very ill', 'He is not going to get better', 'He needs a lot of help now.' House mates and friends could be encouraged to visit, even for a few minutes, perhaps offering to make a drink or bring flowers. Involving them in caring for the person will really help them.

Talking about the illness and dying

'Do I tell him?' 'What do I tell him?' 'How do I tell him?' These are some of the most difficult questions for families and supporters. There is no simple answer. Some people don't want to know, and that should be respected. But most people benefit from clear and straightforward explanations of what is happening to them. Sometimes their situation simply needs to be acknowledged. 'Yes, you are very ill, and it makes you tired', 'No, I don't think your legs will get stronger.' Honesty is needed, even if the question is extremely difficult: 'Am I going to die?' We have often seen how supporters try and make everything sound jolly and cheerful. The person may well respond to such jolliness with a smile, but in fact it often makes them feel confused and lonely inside. They can feel themselves that they are getting weaker, and yet everybody is saying that things are OK.

It is best not to tell any lies, and not to make the person believe that they will get better, if you know that they won't. You also need to consider that the person may want to do certain things, or see certain people, before they die. Ask yourself, 'If he knew he was dying, would he make different choices?'

Understanding the implications of the illness is particularly important if the person needs to make choices about having (or not having) certain medical treatments.

You will need to talk about this together with the other people supporting the person, including their family. If different supporters give the person different messages, that is even more confusing!

Spiritual needs

People have very different ideas about what 'spirituality' means. Some people say it's to do with those aspects of our lives that give life meaning. For some people, their spirituality is expressed through their religion. Spiritual and religious needs often become even more important at the end of life. Spiritual and/or religious needs are not important for everyone, but it's best to check this out if you're not sure. The family usually knows about this. In the book, John and his family want to talk to a priest when John is dying. You could use these pictures to find out what the person you are supporting would like. It may be that they want to see a priest too, or a minister from a different religion, or somebody familiar with the traditions of their own community. Or it may be that they do not want to see anyone, but would like to spend more time listening, for example, to some music which has a special meaning for them.

Getting help

Supporting someone who is dying is too difficult for anyone to do on their own. You must have as much help as possible. The general practitioner (GP) should be able to give advice on what is available. District nurses can offer support with changing medical needs, such as help with managing medication at home. They can also help with equipment such as commodes, hoists and wheelchairs.

Community learning disability teams have a range of professionals (e.g. nurses, social workers, physiotherapists) who can support you, the person and their family/friends in a variety of ways. It will help to contact them at an early stage.

Palliative care teams (sometimes called hospice teams or Macmillan nurses) can give specialist advice and support. They visit patients at home, and can help support them to stay at home, if they want. They help with pain and symptom control, and will be able to talk through any concerns you have, including concerns about how to talk to the person, or how to involve their family. Sometimes the person may be moved to a hospice for treatment and care.

Terminally ill patients can be referred to palliative care teams at any stage of their illness. The teams work with people with any diagnosis, not just cancer. For more information about the help which is available in the UK, see the list of resources at the back of this book.

Guide for healthcare professionals

This book has been designed to help people with learning disabilities who are terminally ill understand what is happening to them. It explains the process of physical deterioration, as well as the emotions involved. The pictures are designed to encourage the person to ask questions and talk about their own symptoms, situation and feelings.

Definition of learning disability

People said to have a 'learning disability' have a reduced ability to understand new or complex information and to learn new skills, and may not be able to cope independently. The condition will have started before adulthood and have a lasting impact on development (based on a definition in *Valuing People*, White Paper, Department of Health, 2001). 'Learning disability' is synonymous with terms used in other countries, such as 'intellectual disability', 'mental handicap' or 'mental retardation'.

Having a learning disability does not mean that the person will never understand the advice or treatment you give. Many people with learning disabilities understand pictures better than words, and have a better visual than written or verbal literacy. Some will have good communication skills, and will not need this book to aid their understanding. A very few will find all information bewildering and will not have the comprehension to follow the sequence of pictures.

Making reasonable adjustments

The Disability Discrimination Act 2005 requires services to make 'reasonable adjustments' to support disabled people to make full use of their service. Caring for patients who have learning disabilities is usually more time-consuming. A person may find it very difficult to be kept waiting. They may need more than one appointment to familiarise themselves with a proposed procedure beforehand. They may need their carer or supporter to be with them in the anaesthetic room and the recovery room before and after a surgical procedure. However, time taken to understand and plan for their special needs usually pays dividends.

Supporters and carers – their role explained

Many people with learning disabilities live at home with their families. Others live alone, with or without support. Some live in residential care settings, like a group home. Many people with learning disabilities will be accompanied to medical appointments by a family member, advocate or staff member whose role it is to support their attendance and communication. Patients often rely much too much on their supporters to help describe their symptoms but the supporters may get them wrong! They may need extra time and encouragement to participate fully in the doctor/ nurse–patient relationship. Sometimes a person with learning disabilities will require a carer to stay with them all the time they are in hospital.

Most supporters need a lot of support themselves when the person they care for is terminally ill. Paid carers in learning disability services are mostly inexperienced and untrained in this area, and don't know what to expect. They may be upset or frightened about what will happen. Even if the patient does not (yet) need your input as a healthcare professional, carers will benefit from an early referral to your service. You may need to spend some extra time with them to give explanations and reassurance.

Consent

Issues of consent are particularly important to consider when there are treatment decisions to be taken. In English law, adults are always presumed to be capable of taking healthcare decisions, unless the opposite has been demonstrated.

It should **never** be assumed that people are not able to make their own decisions, simply because they have a learning disability. Capacity to consent has to be assessed for each decision – someone may be capable of consenting to one aspect of care, but not another. If the person lacks capacity, decisions have to be taken based on what is in the person's **best interest**. Ideally, such decisions should be taken at a 'best interest meeting' with all those involved in the person's care.

There are other key decisions that may not warrant a best interest meeting, such as the decision about where the person is going to be cared for, how they should spend their time, or whether they should be told about their illness. All these questions are likely to worry their carers. It is important to try and involve the person in such decisions as much as possible.

Most people can play a part in deciding how they are going to live and how they are going to die. People with learning disabilities are perfectly able and have a right to make decisions that affect their daily lives and their dying.

Useful resources in the UK

Services

Community Teams for People with Learning Disabilities (CTPLDs)

These are specialist multidisciplinary health teams that support adults with learning disabilities and their families by assessment, by supporting access to mainstream healthcare, and by providing a range of clinical interventions. Your GP or social services department should have the address of the local team.

Organisations to contact for help and advice

Hospice Information Service
Help the Hospices

Hospice House
34–44 Britannia Street
London
WC1X 9JH

Enquiry line: 020 7520 8222
Website:
www.helpthehospices.org.uk/hospiceinformation

Provides information about hospice care and about locally available hospice and palliative care services.

Macmillan Network Information and Support Service

Helpline: 0207 387 3976
Email: info@mniss.co.uk

Provides guidance, information and supoort on caring for people with learning disabilities who have cancer or palliative care needs.

Macmillan Information Line

89 Albert Embankment
London
SE1 7UQ

Helpline: 0808 808 2020
Website: www.macmillan.org.uk

Provides practical, emotional, medical and financial advice for people affected by cancer in general. Also provides information about Macmillan services as well as other cancer organisations and support agencies.

Cruse Bereavement Care

PO Box 800
Richmond
Surrey
TW9 1RG

Helpline: 0844 477 9400
Website: www.cruse.org.uk
Email: helpline@cruse.org.uk

Offers free bereavement counselling, support and information to anyone bereaved by death (including paid carers).

Young person's free helpline: 0808 808 1677
Website: www.rd4u.org.uk
Email: info@rd4u.org.uk

Network for Palliative Care of People with Learning Disabilities

Enquiry line: 0797 726 0967
Email: chair@natnetpald.org.uk

Encourages and contributes to the development of good practice in the palliative care of people with learning disabilities, through networking and organising national and regional study days. Provides information on literature, training and other resources. Open to people from any discipline and to informal carers.

National Council for Palliative Care

The Fitzpatrick Building
188–194 York Way
London
N7 9AS

Telephone: 020 7697 1520
Website: www.ncp.org.uk
Email: enquiries@ncpc.org.uk

Promotes good palliative care for all who need it. Provides good practice guidance for health and social care professionals and influences national strategies. Gives patients and carers opportunities to tell their stories to help shape current practice.

Cancer Black Care

79 Acton Lane
London
NW10 8UT

Telephone: 020 8961 4151

Website: www.cancerblackcare.org
Email: info@cancerblackcare.org

Offers information and advice, and addresses the cultural and emotional needs of Black and other minority ethnic people affected by cancer, as well as their families and friends.

Patient Advice and Liaison Service (PALS)

Website: www.pals.nhs.uk

Mencap Learning Disability Helpline

Telephone: 0808 808 1111

If you have a problem accessing healthcare, speak to the Patient Advice and Liaison Service (PALS) at your local hospital or contact the Mencap Learning Disability Helpline.

Written materials

Caring for People with Learning Disabilities who are Dying

By Noëlle Blackman and Stuart Todd (2005). A clearly written, practical book full of advice for service managers and staff working in learning disability services. Available at £8.99 from Worth Publishing.

Healthcare for All: Independent Inquiry into Access to Healthcare for People with Learning Disabilities

Led by Sir Jonathan Michael, the Inquiry (2008) sought to identify the action needed to ensure adults and children with learning disabilities receive appropriate treatment in acute and primary healthcare in England. The Inquiry report is available as a PDF from www. iahpld.org.uk. Also available in an easy-read version.

The Mental Capacity Act in Practice: Guidance for End of Life Care

Available at £10.00 from the National Council for Palliative Care (www.ncpc.org.uk or on 020 7687 1520).

Loss and Learning Disability

By Noëlle Blackman. This book is for care staff, therapists and counsellors working with people with learning disabilities. It talks about how people with learning disabilities can be affected by bereavement. It includes ways to prevent normal grief from becoming a bigger problem and ways of helping people when the grief process 'goes wrong'. Published by Worth Publishing at £18.99.

The Disability Discrimination Act (DDA) 1995

The Act promotes the civil rights for disabled people and protects them from discrimination. It was significantly extended by the Disability Discrimination Act 2005. You can order an easy-read version on The Stationery Office website (www.tsoshop.co.uk), by phoning them on 0870 600 5522 or by e-mailing them at customer.service@tso.co.uk.

Related titles in the Books Beyond Words series

When Mum Died
When Dad Died

Both by Sheila Hollins and Lester Sireling; illustrated by Beth Webb. Both books take a straightforward and honest approach to death and grief in the family. The pictures tell the story of the death of a parent in a simple but moving way.

When Somebody Dies

By Sheila Hollins, Noelle Blackwood and Sandra Dowling; illustrated by Catherine Brighton. This book shows people with learning disabilities that they need not be alone when they feel sad about someone's death, and that talking about it to a friend or to a counsellor can help them get through this difficult time.

Getting on with Cancer

By Veronica Donaghey, Jane Bernal, Irene Tuffrey-Wijne and Sheila Hollins; ilustrated by Beth Webb. This book tells the story of a woman who is diagnosed with cancer, and then has surgery, radiotherapy and chemotherapy. The book ends on a positive note.

Going to the Doctor

By Sheila Hollins, Jane Bernal, Matthew Gregory; illustrated by Beth Webb. This book illustrates a variety of experiences which may occur at a GP practice. These include meeting the doctor, having one's ears syringed, a physical examination, a blood test, a blood pressure check and getting a prescription.

Going to Out-Patients

By Sheila Hollins, Angie Avis and Samantha Cheverton; illustrated by Denise Redmond. Explains what happens in out-patient departments, covering tests such as ultrasound, X-ray and hearing test. Feelings, information and consent are addressed.

Going into Hospital

By Sheila Hollins, Jane Bernal and Matthew Gregory; illustrated by Denise Redmond. Explains what happens in hospital, covering planned admission for an operation and emergency admission to accident and emergency. Feelings, information and consent are addressed.

Looking after My Breasts

By Sheila Hollins and Wendy Perez; illustrated by Beth Webb. Designed to support women who are invited for breast screening, this book shows a woman having a mammogram and getting a normal result. Another woman demonstrates how to be aware of changes in your own breasts. Feelings, consent and health education are addressed.

Keeping Healthy 'Down Below'

By Sheila Hollins and Jackie Downer; illustrated by Beth Webb. Designed to support women who are invited for a smear test, this book shows a woman making a preliminary visit to her GP practice, deciding whether she will have the smear or not, having it and receiving the results. Feelings, consent and health education are addressed.

Getting on with Epilepsy

By Sheila Hollins, Jane Bernal, Alice Thacker; illustrated by Lisa Kopper. This book illustrates experiences that are worrying for people with epilepsy, like having seizures in public, going to the doctor, having a brain scan, EEG or blood test and taking daily medication. Activities such as safe drinking, swimming and cooking are covered, showing that it is possible to enjoy an active and independent life with epilepsy.

Looking after My Heart

By Sheila Hollins, Francesco Cappuccio and Paul Adeline; illustrated by Lisa Kopper. Jane has enjoyed smoking, drinking alcohol and eating party food over the years. Only when she is taken to hospital after having a heart attack does she begin to look after herself better. She is given medication and advice on preventing further heart disease through eating a healthy diet and taking exercise. In time, she makes a full recovery.

Looking after My Balls

By Sheila Hollins and Justin Wilson; illustrated by Beth Webb. Shows men with learning disabilities how to check their testicles to look for anything that may be wrong and to seek medical help if they are worried.

Enjoying Sport and Exercise

By Sheila Hollins and Caroline Argent; illustrated by Catherine Brighton. Most leisure centres have classes which can be adapted for people with special needs. In this book four people are supported to take up badminton, tai chi, dog walking and playing cricket, and running.

Some other titles in the Books Beyond Words series

Food... Fun, Healthy and Safe

By Sheila Hollins and Margaret Flynn; illustrated by Catherine Brighton. Demonstrates how choosing, cooking and eating food can be fun as well as healthy and safe. Includes do's and don'ts to prevent choking, general advice on eating well and outlines of special diets.

Susan's Growing Up

By Sheila Hollins and Valerie Sinason; illustrated by Catherine Brighton. Susan doesn't understand what is happening to her when she finds blood on her clothes. A teacher explains to her that her periods have started, and her mother takes her shopping to celebrate.

George Gets Smart

By Sheila Hollins, Margaret Flynn and Philippa Russell; illustrated by Catherine Brighton. George likes being with people and doesn't understand why they seem to avoid him. His life changes when he learns to keep clean and smart.

Jenny Speaks Out

By Sheila Hollins and Valerie Sinason; illustrated by Beth Webb. Jenny has been sexually abused and feels unsettled when she moves into a new home in the community. A carer helps her to unravel her painful past and to begin a slow but positive healing process.

Supporting Victims

By Sheila Hollins, Kathryn Stone and Valerie Sinason; illustrated by Catherine Brighton. Polly is the victim of an assault. The man she accuses is arrested. This book shows how she is asked to be a witness at his trial and how the police help her to choose the special measures she needs to give her best evidence. All the special measures available to witnesses are explained.

Books Beyond Words titles are available at £10.00 each. For full details log onto http://www.rcpsych. ac.uk/bbw.

Authors

Sheila Hollins is Professor of Psychiatry of Learning Disability at St George's, University of London.

Irene Tuffrey-Wijne, PhD, has many years' experience in nursing, both in palliative care and learning disabilities. She is a Research Fellow at St George's, University of London.

Lisa Kopper is a distinguished artist and illustrator of children's books. She is well-known for her clear style and ability to draw feelings as well as form.

Acknowledgments

We thank our editorial advisers, Gary Butler, Robert Hill, Nigel Hollins, Marion MacFarlane and Samantha Riches with members of the Squad group in Merton and David Elliott and his group in Staffordshire for their ideas and advice on what was needed in the pictures.

We are grateful for the advice and support of our advisory group which included representatives from the National Council for Palliative Care, Cruse Bereavement Care, the End of Life Care Team at the Department of Health, L'Arche Lambeth, and NHS Wiltshire: Joanna Black, Sarah Bramley Harker, Rosie Dalzell, Vivienne Frankish, Amelia Jones, Lucy Sutton.

We would particularly like to thank Amelia Jones for her advice throughout the development of this book.

Our thanks also to Drs Susan Baker and Sue Read from Staffordshire and Shropshire NHS Trust and the University of Keele for their comments and support.

Finally, we are very grateful to the Department of Health for providing financial support for this project.